OLD GUYS GOLF JOKES

(DON'T GET TEED OFF - LAUGH!)

GREG MARSHALL

OLD GUYS GOLF JOKES

Don't Get Teed Off - LAUGH!

Greg Marshall

Copyright © 2025 by Greg Marshall

All rights reserved.

No part of this book may be reproduced in any form or by any electronic or mechanical means, including information storage and retrieval systems, without written permission from the author, except for the use of brief quotations in a book review.

Dedicated to the memory of my father-in-law

Wiley "Papa" Sims

who loved a good chuckle while playing a round.

Introduction

Golfers *typically* have a great sense of humor.

You'd have to, after driving your ball so far into the woods that Lewis and Clark couldn't find it. Or while staring in disbelief after that short putt somehow lipped the cup. Or while sitting in the clubhouse after your round with your foursome recounting every muffed shot.

Still, those special shots you made keep you coming back, hacking away, determined to improve your game. That and the jokes.

Introduction

Golf jokes are a time-honored golfing tradition, as much as early tee times and a fresh sleeve of golf balls. Old guys enjoy the camaraderie of a match with friends and love to fill the walks or rides between shots with conversation and a laugh or two.

Every bad lie or errant tee shot reminds someone in the group of a story or a one-liner. *"Did you hear the one about…?"*

This book is filled with hilarious golf stories sure to enliven your next round. You'll have fresh material to share on the course and in the clubhouse with a cold one. Or, you can enjoy these in your easy chair recalling your last round with a chuckle. "Been there, done that."

Sit back and enjoy this championship round of golf humor for Old Guys and find the perfect joke to share during your next golf outing.

GOLF STORY JOKES

Chapter 1
A Round of Story Jokes

The Montana State Department of Fish and Wildlife is advising golfers to take extra precautions, and be on the alert for bears while playing on Gallatin, Helena, and Lewis and Clark National Forest's golf courses.

They advise golfers to wear noise-producing devices such as little bells on their clothing to alert, but not to startle the bears unexpectedly.

They also advise golfers to carry pepper spray in the case of an encounter with a bear.

They say that it's also a good idea to watch for signs of bear activity on the courses. They recommend that golfers be educated so that they can recognize the difference between Black bear and Grizzly bear droppings.

Black bear droppings are smaller and contain remains of nuts, berries and possibly squirrel, rabbit or gopher fur.

Grizzly bear droppings have small bells, golf-gloves, sunglasses and other similar golf items in them and they usually smell like pepper spray.

* * *

Two women were playing golf. One teed off and watched in horror as her ball headed directly toward a foursome of men playing the next hole. The ball hit one of the men. He immediately clasped his hands together at his groin, fell to the ground and proceeded to roll around in agony.

The woman rushed down to the man, and immediately began to apologize. "Please allow me to help. I'm a physical therapist and I know I could relieve your pain if you'd allow me," she told him.

"Oh, no, I'll be all right. I'll be fine in a few minutes," the man replied.

It was obvious that he was in agony, lying in the fetal position, still clasping his hands together at his groin.

The female golfer/therapist urged him to let him help him, so at her persistence, he finally allowed her to help.

She gently took his hands away and laid them to his side, loosened his pants and put her hands inside. She administered tender and artful massage to his privates for several long moments and then asked, "How does that feel"?

He replied, "That feels great, but I think my thumb is broken!"

* * *

One fine day, John and Don are out golfing when John slices his ball deep into a wooded ravine. He grabs his 7-iron and proceeds down the embankment into the ravine in search of his ball.

The brush is quite thick, but he searches diligently and suddenly he spots something shiny. As he gets closer, he realizes that the shiny object is in fact a 7-iron in the hands of a skeleton lying near an old golf ball.

John excitedly calls out to his golfing partner: "Hey Don, come here. I've got some real trouble down here."

Don comes running over to the edge of the ravine and calls out: "What's the matter, John? Is everything okay?"

John shouts back in a nervous voice, "Throw me my 8-iron! Apparently, you can't get out of here with a seven.

* * *

A little girl was at her first golf lesson when she asked an interesting question...

Q: "Is the word spelled P-U-T or P-U-T-T?" She asked her instructor.

A: "P-U-T-T is correct," the instructor replied.

"P-U-T means to place a thing where you want it. "P-U-T-T means merely a futile attempt to do the same thing."

* * *

A man was playing his weekly round of golf. He began his round with an eagle on the first hole and a birdie on the second. On the third hole he had just scored his first ever hole in one when his cell phone rang.

It was a doctor notifying him that his wife had just been in a terrible accident and was in critical condition and in the ICU.

The man told the doctor to inform his wife where he was and that the he'd be there as soon as possible. As he hung up he realized he was leaving what was shaping up to be his best ever round so he decided to get in a couple of more holes before heading to the hospital.

He ended up playing all eighteen, finishing his round shooting a personal best 61, shattering the club record by five strokes and beating his previous best score by more than 10. He was jubilant! Then he remembered his wife.

Feeling guilty he dashed to the hospital. He saw the

doctor in the corridor and asked about his wife's condition.

The doctor glared at him and shouted, "You went ahead and finished your round of golf didn't you!?"

"I hope you're proud of yourself! While you were out for the past four hours enjoying yourself at the country club your wife has been languishing in the ICU! It's just as well you went ahead and finished that round because it will be more than likely your last!" "For the rest of her life she will require around the clock care. And you'll be her care giver!"

The man was feeling so guilty he broke down and sobbed uncontrollably.

The doctor laughed and said "I'm just messing with you dude, she's dead. What'd you shoot?"

A man got on a bus, with both of his front pant pockets full of golf balls, and sat down next to a beautiful blonde.

The blonde kept looking quizzically at him and his obviously bulging pants.

Finally, after many such glances from her, he said, "Its golf balls."

The blond looked at him compassionately and said, "Oh you poor thing. I bet that hurts a whole lot worse than tennis elbow?"

***

Two friends were playing golf when one pulled out a cigar but he didn't have a lighter. So, he asked his friend if he had one.

"I sure do," he replied, and reached into his golf bag and pulled out a big 12-inch BIC lighter.

"WOW!" said his friend, "Where did you get that monster?"

"I got it from my genie."

"You have a genie?" the first guy asked.

"Yep, he's right here in my golf bag." He opens his golf bag and out pops a real genie.

The friend says, "I'm a good friend of your master, will you grant me a wish?"

"Yes, I will," the genie replies.

So the friend asks the genie for, "a million bucks."

Done! The genie replied, hops back into the golf bag and leaves the golfers standing there waiting for the "million bucks."

Suddenly the sky begins to darken and a million ducks envelop the golfers.

"Hey," yells to disappointed golfer. "I asked you genie for million bucks, not a million ducks."

"Sorry,' the other golfer replied, "He's hard of hearing,

and besides, do you really think that I'd ask a genie for a 12-inch BIC?"

* * *

A very bad-tempered golfer bought a new set of TaylorMade R7 clubs. After playing with them for a couple of rounds he returned to his pro shop and told the pro, "These were the best clubs I have ever played with. In fact, I can throw these clubs 40-yards further than my old ones!"

* * *

Fred had tried to be particularly careful about his language as he played golf with his preacher. But on the twelfth hole, when he twice failed to hit out of a sand trap, he lost his resolve and let fly with a string of expletives. The preacher felt obliged to respond. "I have observed," said he in a calm voice, "that the best golfers do not use foul language." "I guess not," said Fred, "What the hell do they have to bitch about?"

* * *

A man and his friend meet at the clubhouse and decide to play a round of golf together. The man has a little dog with him and on the first green, when the man holes out a 20-foot putt; the little dog starts to yip and stands up on its hind legs. The friend is quite amazed at this clever trick and says, "That dog is really talented! What does he do if you miss a putt?" "Somersaults," says the man. "Somersaults?" says the friend, "That's incredible. How many does he do?" "Well," says the man. "That depends on how hard I kick him."

A hacker spends a day at a plush country club, playing golf and enjoying the luxury of a complimentary caddy. Being a hacker, he, of course, plays poorly all day. Round about the 18th hole, he spots a lake off to the left of the fairway. He looks at the caddy and says, "I've played so lousy all day, I think I'm going to go drown myself in that lake." The caddy looks back at him and says, "I don't think you could keep your head down that long."

"Caddy, why do you keep looking at your watch?" asked the curious golfer." It's not a watch, sir. It's a compass"

A man walked into the clubhouse and noticed a friend sitting in a corner wearing a neck brace. He sat down and asked his friend what happened. "Well, I was playing golf and I hit my ball into the rough," replied his friend. "Then I met a lady who was looking for her ball too. Finding mine, I thought I'd give her a hand.

There was a cow nearby and I noticed that every time the cow twitched its tail there was a flash of white. So I went over to it and lifted its tail and sure enough there was the ball. I called out to the lady, 'Ma'am, does this look like yours?' And the bitch hit me in the neck with her driver!"

A young golfer was playing in his first PGA Tour event. After his practice round he noticed a beautiful young lady by the clubhouse. He went up to her, began talking, and convinced her to come back to his hotel room for the night. All through the night they made wild love together. In the morning, the woman woke up and arose from bed. The man said, "Please don't go. I love you and I want you to stay with me." The woman replied, "You don't understand...I'm a hooker." The man said, "That's no problem, you probably just have too strong a grip."

The only problem with golf is that the slow people are always in front of you and the fast people always end up behind you.

A fellow caddy and myself recently helped two aged Germans around our course. Failing yet again to get the ball in the air the worst golfer of the pair exclaimed, "I suppose you have never seen any player worse than me?" My friend the caddy replied, "There are plenty worse than you sir but they all quit playing years ago."

* * *

An avid golfer goes to see a fortuneteller to enquire if there are any golf courses in heaven. "I have good news and bad news," she tells the golfer. "What's the good news?" asks the golfer "The good news sir is that the courses in heaven are spectacular, without doubt better than anything you have ever seen on earth." "What's the bad news then?" he asks "You have a tee time at 8:30 tomorrow morning."

* * *

A couple was playing a play-off hole in the annual club championship, and it's down to a very short putt that the wife has to make for the win. She takes her stance, and her husband can see her trembling. She putts and misses and they lose the match. On the way home in the car the husband is fuming, "I can't believe you missed that putt, it was a damn tap in! In fact, it was no longer than my pecker." The wife looked over at her husband and smiled and said, "Yes dear, but it was much harder!"

* * *

A Jew, a Catholic and a Mormon were having drinks at the bar after an interfaith convention. The Jew, bragging about his virility said, "I have four sons, one more and I'll have a basketball team!" The Catholic pooh-poohed that accomplishment, stating, "That's nothing, I have 10 sons, one more and I'll have a football team." To which the Mormon replied, "You fellas ain't got a clue. I have 17 wives, one more and I'll have a golf course!"

A man is stranded on a desert island, all alone for ten years. One day, he sees a speck in the horizon. He thinks to himself, "It's not a ship." The speck gets a little closer and he thinks, "It's not a boat." The speck gets even closer and he thinks, "It's not a raft." Then, out of the surf comes this gorgeous blonde woman, wearing a wet suit and scuba gear. She comes up to the guy and says, "How long has it been since you've had a cigarette?"

"Ten years," he says.

She reaches over and unzips a waterproof pocket on her left sleeve and pulls out a pack of fresh cigarettes.

He takes one, lights it, takes a long drag, and says, "Man, oh man! Is that good!"

Then she asked, "How long has it been since you've had a drink of whiskey?"

He replies, "Ten years!"

She reaches over, unzips her waterproof pocket on her right sleeve, pulls out a flask and gives it to him.

He takes a long swig and says, "Wow, that's fantastic!"

Then she starts unzipping a longer zipper that runs down the front of her wet suit and she says to him, "And how long has it been since you've had some real fun?"

And the man replies, "Wow! Don't tell me that you've got golf clubs in there!"

After a particularly poor round of golf, a popular club member skipped the clubhouse and started to go home. As he was walking to the parking lot to get his car, a policeman stopped him and asked, "Did you tee off on the sixteenth hole about twenty minutes ago?"

"Yes," the golfer responded.

"Did you happen to hook your ball so that it went over the trees and off the course?"

"Yes, I did. How did you know?" he asked.

"Well," said the policeman very seriously, "Your ball flew out onto the highway and crashed through a driver's windshield. The car went out of control, crashing into five other cars and a fire truck. The fire truck couldn't make it to the fire, and the building burned down. So, what are you going to do about it?"

The golfer thought it over carefully and responded...

"I think I'll close my stance a little bit, tighten my grip and lower my right thumb."

* * *

Husband and wife were playing in the club's mixed foursomes. He hit a great drive down the middle – she sliced the second shot into a copse of trees. Unfazed he played a brilliant recovery shot, which went onto the green a foot from the pin. She poked at the putt and sent it ten feet beyond the pin. He lined up the long putt and sank it. To his wife he said, "We'll have to do better. That was a bogey five." "Don't blame me," she snapped, "I only took two of them."

* * *

The Englishman's wife steps up to the tee and, as she bends over to place her ball, a gust of wind blows her skirt up and reveals her lack of underwear. "Good God, woman! Why aren't you wearing any undies?" her husband demanded.

"Well, you don't give me enough housekeeping money to afford any."

The Englishman immediately reaches into his pocket and says, "For the sake of decency, here's $20. Go and buy yourself some underwear.

"Next, the Irishman's wife bends over to set her ball on the tee. Her skirt also blows up to show that she too is wearing no undies. "Blessed Virgin Mary, woman! You've no undies. Why not?"

She replies, "I can't afford any on the money you give me."

He reaches into his pocket and says, "For the sake of decency, here's $10. Go and buy yourself some underwear!"

Lastly, the Scotsman's wife bends over. The wind also takes her skirt over her head to reveal that she, too, is naked under it. "Sweet muddier of Jesus, Aggie! Where are yer drawers?"

She too explains, "You dinna give me enough money ta be able ta affarrd any." The Scotsman reaches into his pocket and says, "Well, fer the love 'o Jesus, here's a comb. Tidy yerself up a bit."

During the weekly Lamaze class, the instructor emphasized the importance of exercise, hinting strongly that husbands need to get out and start walking with their wives. From the back of the room one expectant father inquired, "Would it be okay if she carries a bag of golf clubs while she walks?"

A man was golfing one day and was struck by lightning. He died and went to heaven. Saint Peter told him when he arrived at the gates of heaven that the bolt of lightning was actually meant for his golf partner. But, because God doesn't want it known that he makes mistakes, so the man would have to go back to earth as someone other that himself. Well, the man thought about it for a while and announced to Saint Peter that he wanted to return to earth as a lesbian. Saint Peter asked the man why a macho guy like him would choose to return as a lesbian. The man answered, "It's simple really, this way I can still make love to a woman, AND I can hit from the red tees!"

A couple whose passion had waned saw a marriage counselor and went through a number of appointments that brought little success. Suddenly at one session the counselor grabbed the wife and kissed her passionately. "There" he said to the husband, "That's what she needs every Monday, Wednesday, Saturday and Sunday". "Well," replied the husband, "I can bring her in on Mondays and Wednesdays but Saturdays and Sundays are my golf days."

* * *

"Tom" sits in clubhouse bar thinking about his next extra marital affair. Deep in thought about the subject, he absentmindedly starts thinking aloud. "Not worth it," he muttered. "Never as good as you hoped. Expensive and above all, drives the wife berserk." A friend who was sitting close by at the time and overheard Tom's words leaned across and said, "Come on Tom, you knew what to expect when you took up golf."

Mike and Bob had just finished the front nine and it was obvious that Mike was having a bad day. "Gee Mike, you're just not your old self today, what's the matter?" asked Bob. Mike, looking pretty glum, said, "I think Mabel's dead." "Damn, that's terrible," said Bob, "You sat you 'think' your wife is dead. Aren't you sure?" "Well," responded Mike, "The sex is the same, but the dishes are piling up."

I was recently playing a round of golf with a nice young fellow. On the first hole, which was a long par four with water to the right and a deep ravine to the left, the young man took out a brand new sleeve of balls, teed one up and immediately hit it into the water on the right. Undaunted, he pulled another ball from the sleeve and hit that one into the ravine, as well. Then he took the last ball from the sleeve and hit it, too, into the water. He then reached into his bag and pulled out another brand new sleeve of balls. "Why don't you hit an old ball?" I asked. He responded, "I've never had an old ball."

* * *

A priest is playing a round of golf at the local public course when he arrives at the 15th tee. This hole is a 160-yard par three with a lake in the front of the green. It is also the padre's nemesis, no matter how well or how poorly he is playing.

Upon arriving at the tee, the priest tees up his ball, gets ready to hit and, at the last minute, looks toward the heavens and says, "God, I have been a good and decent man. Please, just this once, let me hit a shot which will carry the lake and get onto the green."

As he is about to swing, a loud, deep voice booms from the heavens and says, "Use a new ball, they go farther."

The preacher steps back, thinks about the heavenly advice and goes to his bag and gets a brand new ball. He takes his stance and once again the heavenly voice booms, "Take a practice swing first."

The preacher is now awestruck by the heavenly advice, so he steps back from the ball and takes a practice swing.

He takes his stance and gets ready to hit and the heavenly voice booms, "Use the old ball."

* * *

A couple had a whirlwind, 30-day romance and even though they don't know too much about each other, they decide to get married. After a couple weeks, the husband says, "Honey, I have something I have to tell you. I'm a golf fanatic and I must play every day."

"I also need to tell you something," she replies. "I'm a hooker, and I need to do it every day."

"That's OK," he said, "we'll just play dog leg lefts."

Two pastors, one Catholic and one Protestant, and a Jewish rabbi were part of a threesome one day on the course. The groups ahead of them was playing slow, terrible golf and weren't gesturing for a play-through. After several holes of this agonizingly slow golf the three clerics began to get very impatient, each muttering his own curses upon the group ahead of them. Soon the Marshall came around, and was hailed down by the holy men who shouted, "We're sick of being held-up by these yahoos ahead of us who won't allow us to play through!"

The Marshall stated, "I'm sorry, gentlemen, but those men are both deaf and blind."

The Protestant cried, "Oh, Jesus, forgive me for my bad thoughts and cursing upon those poor souls."

The Catholic cried, "Oh forgive me, Mary, for my bad thoughts and cursing upon those poor souls."

The rabbi shouted, "So why can't they play at night!?"

* * *

The duffer decided that it was about time for a lesson to "tune up" his game. He told the pro that he wanted to work on swing mechanics, so the pro asked him to hit a few balls with his 9-iron so he could watch his swing. He addressed the ball, double-checked his stance and grip, executed his take-away and backswing, his downswing and follow through. But, he toed the ball, and sliced it way off into the nearest fairway. He looked back at the pro for advice, who told him "Your problem is obvious Sir — it's LOFT."

The golfer scratched his head, went to his bag and pulled out his driver. He repeated his routine, and topped the ball, sending it dribbling 30 yards out on the practice range. He looked at the pro for a suggestion, who advised him "Your problem is still LOFT."

The frustrated student then pulled out a 5-iron, took his swing and struck an ugly duck hook. The pro again told him "I'm sorry, but your problem is still LOFT."

The golfer struggled to maintain his cool, and asked the pro, "I don't understand. I hit my first shot with my 9-iron, and you said my problem was loft. Then I took my least lofted club, hit it again, and you said my problem was still loft. Then I grabbed a middle iron, and you told me once again that my problem was loft. What exactly do mean by LOFT?"

The pro looked at him and explained, "L.O.F.T. – Lack Of Freaking Talent!"

* * *

It seems there was this priest who just loved to play golf, but he had been very busy for many months and had not been able to get away to go golfing. Well, one Sunday morning he woke up and felt he just HAD to go golfing. The weather was just beautiful.

He called up the Bishop and claimed he had a really bad case of laryngitis and couldn't preach, so the Bishop told him to rest for several days. He then got out his clubs and headed off for the golf course.

He set up at the first hole, making sure no one was there to see him playing hooky, and blasted the ball with his wood. It was a beautiful shot! It went straight and true. It bounced, and bounced (right up onto the green) and rolled its way closer... and closer... a hole-in-one! The priest jumped up and down in his excitement, praising the Lord and shouting hallelujahs!

He struts off to the green, collects his ball, and tees off at the second hole, repeating his performance on the first hole, much to his astounded delight.

All this time St. Peter and God have been watching him from the gates of heaven. St. Peter has finally seen enough to pique his curiosity. "Lord," he says, "this priest seems to be a real trouble maker. He ignored his congregation and even lied to go golfing. Now you reward him with a hole-in-one! Why?"

God smiles, looks over at St. Peter, and says, "I'm punishing him." St. Peter looks very confused and asks God for an explanation. God replies, "Well, after he finishes his game by himself, who's he gonna tell about it?"

* * *

A man got a phone call from his wife at work one day and she asked him to stop at the store and pick up some groceries. Reminding her that this was his golf league day, he said he would be happy to go to the store AFTER playing his round of golf.

After playing golf, he stopped at the store and picked up 2 bags full of groceries. He then proceeded to walk out of the grocery store to his Cadillac. Upon reaching his Cadillac he found it difficult to reach into his pocket to pull his keys out to open his trunk because his arms were full with two bags of groceries. He saw a beautiful women walking nearby and he asked her, "Could you please do me a favor?"

"Sure," she replied.

He went on to say, "I can't reach into my pocket and get my Cadillac keys out to open my trunk and put my groceries away." "Do you think you could reach into my pocket and pull my Cadillac keys out?"

"No problem," she replied.

When she pulled the keys out, two golf tees also were pulled out as well and fell to the ground. She bent over and picked them up. Looking at the golf tees in the palm of her hand, somewhat quizzically she asked the man, "Gee, what are these for?" He replied, "Oh, those are to keep my balls in the air while I'm driving."

To which she commented, "Boy, those Cadillac engineers think of everything."

* * *

A terrible golfer was playing a round of golf for which he had hired a caddie. The round proved to be somewhat tortuous for the caddie to watch and he was getting a bit exasperated by the poor play of his employer.

At one point the ball lay about 180-yards from the green and the as the golfer sized up his situation, he asked his caddie, "Do you think I can get there with a 5-iron?"

To which the caddie replied, "Eventually."

* * *

A golfer was hitting a ball from the first hole in front of the clubhouse. The ball was sitting about 2-feet in front of the tee markers. The golfer approached the ball with his wood, setup silently, and was ready to swing when, over the loudspeaker, the voice of the pro from the clubhouse said," Would the gentleman on the first tee please tee his ball behind the tee markers for his first shot."

The voice broke the man's concentration, and he backed away, came up to the ball again, set up, and was again ready to hit. The voice over the loudspeaker repeated, "Would the gentleman on the first tee PLEASE tee up his ball behind the tee markers for his first shot."

The golfer backed away, strolled up to the starter and said, "Would you please tell the gentleman in the clubhouse that the gentleman on the first tee is hitting his second shot?"

Two friends were playing golf one day. They decided that they would adhere strictly to the rules, i.e., no mulligans, improving their lies, etc. After a few holes, one guy's ball landed on a cart path. As he reached down to pick up his ball to get relief his friend said, "We agreed that we would not improve our lie."

No matter how much the first fellow tried to explain that he was entitled to this relief, the second fellow would not allow it.

To the man went to the cart to get a club. As he stood over the ball he took a few practice swings, each time scraping the club on the pavement, taking out big chunks of blacktop and sending out lots of sparks! Finally, after several practice swings, he took his shot. The ball took off and landed on the green about 6-feet from the pin.

"Great shot!" his friend exclaimed. "What club did you use?" The man answered, "I used YOUR 7-iron!!!!!"

***

Jesus and Moses were playing golf one day. They arrived at a tough, 215-yard par three, all over water. Jesus had the honor and stepped up to the tee with a 4 iron. Moses tried to convince him that it wasn't the right club, "That's not enough club; you need at least a 4 wood."

Jesus responded, "No, I saw Arnold Palmer play this hole the other day and he put a 4-iron five feet from the pin and sank the putt for a birdie." Moses said, "I'm telling you, that's not enough club!"

Jesus hit the ball into the water. He parted the water, walked out and got the ball, smoothed out the water and teed up again. Moses said, "I told you that was not enough club; you need at least a 4 wood."

Jesus said, "This will be fine — remember what I said about Arnold Palmer." Jesus hit the ball into the water one more time. As Moses looked on in disgust, Jesus got his ball and teed it up for yet another try.

About that time the next foursome was approaching the tee and one of the golfers in the new foursome said, "What's he doing hitting a 4 iron on this hole? He needs at least a 4 wood. Who does he think he is - Jesus?" "No," replied Moses, "He thinks he's Arnold Palmer!"

***

A funeral procession was driving by the golf course as a group was putting on the 18th green. Upon seeing the hearse, one of the players stopped and put his hat over his heart as the procession passed. "That was really a very nice gesture," one of his buddies said. "Hey, it's the least I could do. Sunday would have been our 35th wedding anniversary!"

* * *

A man and his wife were playing golf with another couple at their club. They came to a par 4, dogleg left. The man pulled his drive to the left and left it behind a storage barn. His friend said, "If you open the front door and the back door of the barn, you'll have a clear shot to the green." So they opened the doors and the man took his shot. It rattled through the rafters of the barn, shot out through a window, hit his wife on the head and killed her!

It was ten years before the man could get the courage to play the course again. Sure enough, he got to the same hole, pulled his drive again and ended up behind the same storage barn. The man he was playing with this time said, "If you open the front door and the back door of the barn, you'll have a clear shot to the green." The man said, "I don't think so. The last time I tried that, it was the worst day of my life." "Really? What happened?" asked his friend. The man replied, "I took a nine on this hole!"

* * *

There was a threesome of men warming up on the first tee at Pebble Beach, when a very pretty young woman came up and asked if she could join them in their round. They asked what her handicap was and she told them it was a 4. They said they'd be happy to have her join the group and she told them how she had always wanted to play Pebble Beach and what a very special day this was for her.

When the round began it quickly became clear that she was quite a good golfer. She hit the ball beautifully and she showed exceptional skill in all aspects of the game. Throughout the round she told the other members of the group that it had been her life-long dream to play Pebble Beach and to have a great round. She certainly was doing that, as after 17 holes she was at even par for the day.

She teed off and hit a terrific drive right down the middle of the fairway. Her second shot landed on the green about four and a half feet from the pin — but it was a very difficult, side-hill lie. She studied her putt for a few moments, then she walked over to where the men were observing. "You know," she said, "this is a very special day for me. I've always wanted to have a great round at Pebble Beach and now I have the chance to birdie the course. This really means a lot to me, and if any of you can tell me the best way to sink this putt, there's thirty minutes of the best sex you've ever had in your life in it for you!"

Well, the first man ran over and said, "You know, I had this exact putt about two weeks ago and I can tell you that the best way to putt it is to hit it hard about 5-inches above the cup."

The second man pushed him out of the way and said, "No way! I've had this putt many times and I know that the best thing to do is to hit it soft about 10-inches high of the cup."

The third man walked up and said, "Don't listen to either of them." He then picked up her ball and handed it to her and said, "That's a gimme!"

So there's this guy who golfs with his buddies every weekend, and his wife keeps bugging him to take her along and teach her to play. He finally relents, and the following Sunday finds them on the first tee.

She's never played, so he tells her to go down to the ladies tees, watch him drive, and then try to do like he did. She goes down to the reds, the guy hooks his drive, and the ball hits his wife, killing her.

The police come to investigate, and the coroner says, "It's the damnedest thing I ever saw. There's an imprint on her temple, and you can read "Titleist 1."

"That was my ball," the guy said.

"What I don't understand," the coroner continued, "is the one on her hip that says "Titleist 3."

"Oh," the guy replied, "that was my mulligan."

* * *

A man was playing 18 holes by himself. On the 15th tee he hooked his ball into some buttercups along the left of the fairway. Being an honorable man, he penalized himself one stroke and moved his ball out of the pretty flowers.

Then a fairy appeared. She said "Thank you for moving your ball out of the earth's beautiful buttercups, you will now be blessed with an unlimited supply of butter for the rest of your life!"

"Well, thanks," the man replied, "but where were you yesterday when I hit my ball into the pussy willows?"

* * *

It seems that there was this Chinese businessman visiting a newly acquired business in the United States. As a gesture of good will, the executives of his newly acquired business took him to a golf course for a round of golf. He had never played the game before.

Upon his return to China, his family asked what he had done in the United States. He replied, "Played most interesting game. Hit little white ball with long stick in large cow pasture. Name of game is Oh, shit."

* * *

Dear Abby,

I've never written to you before, but I really need your advice.

I have suspected for some time now that my wife has been cheating on me. The usual signs: phone rings, but if I answer, the caller hangs up. My wife has been going out with "the girls" a lot recently, although when I ask their names she always says, "Just some friends from work, you don't know them."

I always try to stay awake to look out for her coming home, but I usually fall asleep. Anyway, I have never broached the subject with my wife. I think deep down I just didn't want to know the truth, but last night she went out again and I decided to really check on her.

Around midnight, I decided to hide in the garage behind my golf clubs so I could get a good view of her when she arrived home from a night out with "the girls". When she got out of the car she was buttoning up her blouse and she took her panties out of her purse and slipped them on. It was at that moment, crouching behind my clubs, that I noticed that the graphite shaft on my driver appeared to have a hairline crack right by the club head.

Is this something I can fix myself or should I take it back to the pro shop where I bought it?

Signed,

Perplexed

* * *

There was a good man named Bill who died and appeared before St. Peter at the Holy Gates. St. Peter checks out his books and discovers that there is a problem. He says that there is no clear answer in the books on where the man is supposed to go, Heaven or Hell. He suggests that the man should go to Hell and check it out, so that he may make the decision himself. If he didn't like what he saw there, he could come back to Heaven.

Well, this man had only one true vice while he was alive. It seems he had an uncontrollable desire to play golf at any opportunity. He had traveled the world playing all the famous golf courses. When the man arrived in Hell, Satan welcomed him, but he too was surprised at the man's situation. He had assumed that since the question about the man's ultimate destination wasn't clear, the man would go to Heaven.

Behind Satan, Bill could see the most beautiful golf course ever built. It had beautiful trees, blue ponds, water separating the fairways, and almost everything in a golf course a golfer could ever wish for in life. Bill fell in love with it at first sight, and he couldn't control himself. He just had to play a round. The devil showed him a solid gold electric golf cart, and a perfect set of custom clubs. Satan reached into his pocket and presented the man with a Golden Tee. The devil then said that only members could play. The man couldn't control himself. He just had to play there.

Bill returns to Heaven and tells St. Peter that he has decided to stay in Hell so he could play on the

Beautiful Golf Course there. When the man returns to Hell, he approaches Satan and asks for a tee time. The devil says that anytime at all, the man could play. No one else uses the course. Chuckling with glee, the man approaches the first tee. He gets out of his beautiful golf cart, reaches for his perfectly matched clubs and selects his driver. He then reaches into his pants pocket and pulls out his Golden Tee, then frantically searches everywhere for a ball. Satan comes up and the Bill asks him for a ball.

"That's the Hell of it," says Satan.

A deaf mute steps up to tee off on the first hole of a golf course, when a large burly guy yells "Hey You!, Nobody tees off ahead of Big Ralph". Being deaf the poor guy continues to prepare for his shot, so Ralph runs up thinking the deaf mute is being obstinate, and knocks the poor guy to the ground, kicks his ball away, and prepares for his own shot. After Ralph has hit the ball and proceeded down the fairway after it, the mute gets up brushes himself off, waits a moment, and again prepares his shot.

The deaf mute then hits a beautiful shot straight up the middle of the fairway, striking big Ralph in the back of the head, and knocking him unconscious. The mute then walks down the fairway rolls big Ralph and holds up four fingers in front of Ralph's face.

* * *

A woman has just finished playing the first hole, and is walking to the second when she is stung by a bee. She runs back to the pro shop, and tells the pro..."i was just stung by a bee!!"

The pro inquires..."Where were you stung?"

She replies..."Between the first and second holes!!"

The pro thinks for a moment, and says..."Well, there's your problem - your stance is too wide!"

An American citizen is vacationing on his own in Ireland. He decides to play a round and is paired with three locals. He takes a few practice swings, steps up to the first tee, and proceeds to hook the ball out of bounds. He shakes his head, reaches in his pocket, and re-tees another ball. He tells his playing partners that he is taking a mulligan. He pounds one down the center of the fairway.

With a big smile, he asks the others, "In the States, we call that a mulligan. What do you call it here in Ireland?" After a moment of silence, one of the locals replies, "Hitting three."

John and Bob were two of the bitterest rivals at the club. Neither man trusted the other's scorekeeping. One day they were playing a heated match and watching each other like hawks. After holing out on the fourth green and marking his six on the scorecard, John asked Bob, "What'd you have?"

Bob went through the motions of mentally counting up. "Six!" he said and then hastily corrected himself – " No, no.... a five."

Calmly John marked the scorecard, saying out loud "Eight!" "Eight?" Bob said, "I couldn't have had eight."

John said, "Nope, you claimed six, then changed it to five, but actually you had seven."

"Then why did you mark down eight?" asked Bob.

John told him, "One stroke penalty, for improving your lie."

Nick and Lou head out for a quick round of golf. Since they're short on time, they decide to play only 9 holes. Nick says to Lou, "Let's say we make the time worth the while, at least for one of us, and spot $5 on the lowest score for the day."

Lou agrees and they enjoy a great game. After the 8th hole, Lou is ahead by one stroke, but slices his ball into the rough on the 9th. "Help me find my ball; you look over there," he says to Nick.

After three minutes, neither has had any luck. Since a lost ball carries a two-stroke penalty, Lou pulls a ball from his pocket and tosses it to the ground. "I've found my ball!" he announces triumphantly.

Nick looks at him forlornly, "After all the years we've been friends, you'd cheat me on golf for a measly five bucks?"

"What do you mean cheat? I found my ball sitting right here!"

"And a liar, too!" Nick says with amazement. "I'll have you know I've been standing on your ball for the last three minutes!"

A golfer sliced a ball into a field of chickens, striking one of the hens and killing it instantly. He was understandably upset and sought out the farmer. "I'm sorry," he said, "my terrible tee-shot hit one of your hens and killed it. Can I replace the hen?"

"I don't know about that," replied the farmer, mulling it over. "How many eggs a day do you lay?"

A young man with a few hours to spare one afternoon figures that if he hurries and plays very fast, he can get in nine holes before he has to head home. As he is about to tee off, an old gentleman shuffles onto the tee and asks if he can join him. Although worried this will slow him up, the younger man says, "Of course." To his surprise, the old man plays quickly. He doesn't hit the ball very far, but it goes straight. Furthermore, the old man moves along without wasting any time.

When they reach the 9th fairway, the young man is facing a tough shot. A large pine tree sits in front of his ball, directly between it and the green. After several minutes of pondering how to hit the shot, the old man says, "You know, when I was your age, I'd hit the ball right over that tree." With the challenge before him, the young man swings hard, hits the ball, watches it fly into the branches, rattle around, and land with a thud a foot from where it had started.

"Of course," says the old man, "when I was your age, that tree was only three feet tall."

Moral of the Story? Never trust an Old Guy.

Alex and Jim are trying to get in a quick 18 holes, but there are two terrible lady golfers in front of them hitting the ball everywhere but where it's supposed to go.

Alex comments to Jim, 'Why don't you go over and ask if we can play through?' Jim gets about halfway there, turns, and comes back so Alex asks, 'What's wrong?'

Jim replies, 'One of them is my wife, and the other is my mistress.' Alex responds, 'That could be a problem. I'll go over and have a word.'

He gets about halfway there and he turns and comes back, too. So Jim says, 'What's wrong?'

Alex murmurs, 'Small world.'

* * *

Noting that her husband looked more haggard and disgruntled than usual after his weekly golf game, his wife asked what was wrong.

He answered, "Well, on the 4th hole, Harry had a heart attack and died. It was terrible! The entire rest of the day, it was hit the ball, drag Harry, hit the ball, drag Harry!"

* * *

Martin and his wife Debbie, walk into a dentist's office. Martin says to the dentist, "Doc, I'm in one heck of a hurry. I have three buddies sitting out in my car waiting for us to play golf, so forget about the anesthetic, I don't have time for the gums to get numb. I just want you to pull the tooth, and be done with it! Today's Friday and we have a 10:00 AM tee time at the best golf course in town and it's 9:15 already... "

The dentist thought to himself, "My goodness, this is surely a very brave man asking to have a tooth pulled without using anything to kill the pain." So the dentist asks Martin, "Which tooth is it, Sir?"

Martin turned to his wife and said, "Open your mouth and show him, dear..."

* * *

After they went into the locker room, another golfer who had heard the old guys talking about their game went to the pro and asked, "I've been playing golf for a long time and thought I knew all the terminology of the game, but what's a rider?"

The pro said, "A rider is when you hit the ball far enough to actually get in the golf cart and ride to it."

ONE-LINERS AND PUNS

Chapter 2
A Chip Shot of One Liners And Puns

"I once played a course that was so tough, I lost two balls in the ball washer!"

* * *

"I had a terrible round today," the golfer told his wife. "I only hit two good balls, and that was when I stepped on a rake in the sand trap."

* * *

An interesting thing about golf is that no matter how badly you play, it's always possible to get worse.

* * *

Golf is a game invented by God to punish people who retire early.

* * *

I like big putts and I cannot lie.

* * *

There are three ways to improve your golf score: take lessons, practice constantly... or start cheating.

* * *

Why do golf announcers whisper? Because they don't want to wake up the people watching.

* * *

I play in the low 80s. If it's any hotter than that, I won't play.

* * *

Golf: a 5-mile walk punctuated with disappointments.

* * *

If your opponent can't remember if he shot a six or a seven on a hole, chances are he had an eight on it.

* * *

In primitive society, when native tribes beat the

ground with clubs and yelled, it was called witchcraft; today, in civilized society, it's called golf.

Golf can best be defined as an endless series of tragedies obscured by the occasional miracle.

To some golfers, the greatest handicap is the ability to add correctly.

Golf was once a rich man's sport, but now it has millions of poor players!

The difference between a whiff and a practice swing - no one curses after a practice swing.

* * *

You should always try before you buy, especially when buying a putter. Never buy a putter until you've seen how well you can throw it.

The higher the handicap of the golfer, the more likely it is that he'll be telling you what you should be doing to fix your game.

* * *

Golf brings out the 3-year-old in us – we struggle to count past 5.

* * *

Golf balls are like eggs. They're both white, sold by the dozen, and a week later you have to go out and buy more.

* * *

Golf is what you play when you're too out of shape to play other sports.

* * *

Golf was once a rich man's sport, but now it has millions of poor players!

* * *

Where can you find a golfer on a Saturday night? Clubbing!

* * *

If I hit it right, it's a slice. If I hit it left, it's a hook. If I hit it straight, it's a miracle.

* * *

In golf, you can hit a 2-acre fairway 10-percent of the time, but hit a 2-inch branch 90-percent of the time.

* * *

The game of golf is 90-percent mental and 10-percent mental.

* * *

Golfer: That can't be my ball, it looks too old.

Caddie: It's been a long time since we started.

* * *

A good golf partner is one who's always a little bit worse than you are.

* * *

A "gimme" can best be defined as an agreement between two golfers... neither of whom can putt very well.

* * *

Golf is an odd game! You hit down to make the ball go up. You swing left and the ball goes right. The lowest score wins. And on top of that, the winner buys the drinks

* * *

What are the four worst words you could hear during a game of golf? "It's still your turn!"

* * *

Many a golfer prefers a golf cart to a caddy because it cannot count, criticize, or laugh.

* * *

The worst day on the course is better than your best day in the office.

* * *

What did Master Yoda say when Luke sliced the ball onto the next fairway over? "May the 'Fores' be with you..."

* * *

"My doctor told me I can't play golf."

"Oh, when did he play with you?"

* * *

The most redundant thing on a golf course is a ball-washer on a hole with water hazards.

* * *

"My wife said I play so much golf it's driving a wedge between us."

* * *

"I came home to my wife in lingerie… she said I could tie her up and do whatever I wanted. So I tied her to the chair and went to the driving range."

* * *

Which pro golfers can jump higher than the flag?

All of them…. the flag can't jump…

* * *

I told my buddy I got a new set of clubs for my wife. He said, "Sounds like a good trade!"

* * *

What do you call a lion playing golf? Roarin' McIlroy

* * *

Why did Tarzan spend so much time on the golf course?

He was perfecting his swing.

* * *

I hate golf courses with too many trees, I go to great links to avoid them.

* * *

When golfers make golf jokes – Are they just meta-fores?

* * *

Who's the best person at the golf course to get to make coffee?

The groundskeeper!

* * *

How many golfers does it take to change a light bulb?

FORE!

* * *

I'm not a bad putter, I just can't catch a break.

* * *

What type of golf game did the fur traders play in the old days?

A skins match.

* * *

Golfer A: I played World War II golf—out in 39 and home in 45. **Golfer B:** I played Civil War golf—out in 61 and home in 65.

* * *

Is he a bad golfer? I'll tell you how bad he is. In his bag he carries flares, a compass and emergency rations.

* * *

The way he plays they should put the flags on the greens at half-mast.

* * *

It seems to me that at times the hardest thing about golf is being allowed out of the house to play it.

* * *

It's a strange world isn't it? You hire someone to mow your lawn, so that you'll have time to play golf for the exercise.

* * *

He's too fat to play. If he places the ball where he can hit it, he can't see it. If he places it where he can see it, he can't hit it.

* * *

Real golfers have two handicaps: one for braggin' and one for bettin'.

* * *

Real golfers don't cry when they line up their fourth putt.

* * *

What's the difference between a bad golfer and a bad skydiver? A bad golfer goes: WHACK..."Damn!" A bad Skydiver goes: "Damn!"...WHACK.

* * *

How's golf like fishing?

Both mysteriously encourage exaggeration.

CELEBRITY GOLF JOKES AND QUOTES

Chapter 3
A Clubhouse Full of Celebrity Golf Jokes And Quotes

"I have a tip that can take five strokes off anyone's game: It's called an eraser." - *Arnold Palmer*

* * *

"If you drink, don't drive. Don't even putt." - *Dean Martin*

* * *

"It took me seventeen years to get three thousand hits in baseball. It took one afternoon on the golf course." - *Hank Aaron*

* * *

"You've just got one problem. You stand too close to the ball after you've hit it." - *Sam Snead*

* * *

"We learn so many things from golf – how to suffer, for instance." - *Bruce Lansky*

* * *

"If you are caught on a golf course during a storm and are afraid of lightning, hold up a 1-iron. Not even God can hit a 1-iron" - *Lee Trevino*

* * *

"If you watch a game, it's fun. If you play at it, it's recreation. If you work at it, it's golf." - *Bob Hope*

* * *

"Golf is a game in which you yell four, shoot six, and write down five." - *Paul Harvey*

* * *

"Pressure is when you play $5 a hole with only $2 in your pocket." - *Lee Trevino*

* * *

"The income tax has made more liars out of the American people than golf has." - *Will Rogers*

* * *

"Give me the fresh air, a beautiful partner, and a nice round of golf, and you can keep the fresh air and the round of golf." - Jack Benny

* * *

"Golf is a game invented by the same people who think music comes out of a bagpipe" - *Lee Trevino*

* * *

"It's good sportsmanship to not pick up lost golf balls while they are still rolling." - *Mark Twain*

* * *

"I don't say my golf game is bad, but if I grew tomatoes they'd come up sliced." - *Arnold Palmer*

* * *

"If you are going to throw a club, it is important to throw it ahead of you, down the fairway, so you don't have to waste energy going back to pick it up." - *Tommy Bolt*

* * *

"If a lot of people gripped a knife and fork as poorly as they do a golf club, they'd starve to death." - *Sam Snead*

***

"The only sure rule in golf is he who has the fastest golf cart never has to play the bad lie." - *Mickey Mantle*

***

"I know I am getting better at golf because I am hitting fewer spectators." - *Gerald Ford*

***

"Golf is a good walk spoiled." - *Mark Twain*

***

"Golf is a puzzle without an answer. I've played the game for 40 years and I still haven't the slightest idea how to play." - *Gary Player*

***

"I would like to deny all allegations by Bob Hope that during my last game of golf, I hit an eagle, a birdie, an elk and a moose." - *Gerald Ford*

***

"Golf tips are like aspirin. One may do you good, but if you swallow the whole bottle you will be lucky to survive." - *Harvey Penick*

* * *

"It's alive, this swing, a living sculpture! And down through contact, always down, striking the ball crisply, with character. A tuning fork goes off in your heart and your balls." - *Roy McAvoy (Tin Cup)*

* * *

"I play golf with friends sometimes, but there are never friendly games." - *Ben Hogan*

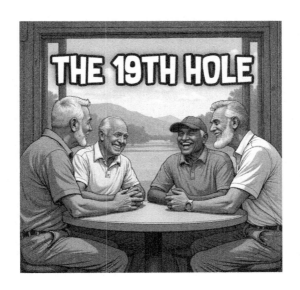

We conclude our collection with a joke for every Old Guy golfer who has thought better of heading out to play during inclement weather. I hope you've enjoyed the laughs - see you on the next tee!

An Old Guy husband wakes up at 5 a.m. and rolls out of bed to get ready to head to the golf course for his 6:30 tee time. He gets dressed and opens the garage door and starts backing out and he notices that it's raining pretty hard. There's lightning flashing in the sky and the ominous dark clouds stretch as far as the eye can see.

He thinks about it for a few minutes and then decides not to go. He pulls the car back into the garage and he goes and sits in the living room and watches TV for about an hour. He finally decides to go back upstairs, gets into bed slowly to not wake up the wife and he kisses her shoulder and he says "It's raining really hard outside".

The wife doesn't roll over but says, "Yeah, and can you believe it - my idiot husband went golfing!"

About the Author

Greg Marshall is a card-carrying Old Guy who enjoys a good tale as much as the next Old Guy. He spends his days collecting jokes, puns, and one-liners to share with others. (And he has played some less than stellar golf.)

He also writes recollections of days gone by that do homage to sweet memories, and tries to find the humor and good in make the less than sweet ones more palatable.

Also by Greg Marshall

Visit his "Pepper's Books" Author Page on Amazon for the full selection of his books that are available. There are books for children and adults alike, including these popular joke books for "Old Guys", "Dad Joke" aficionados, and committed Punsters.

Old Guys Joke Book: A New Wrinkle On Humor

Old Guys Joke Book: A Second Helping

I'm Here All Week (Try The Veal)

I'm Here All Week (Try The Veal) - Encore Performance

Attack of the Killer Dad Jokes

Have grandkids or nieces and nephews that love to laugh?

Hilarious Jokes For Kids!

Printed in Great Britain
by Amazon